Date: 8/27/14

COMMUNITY · CONNECTIONS

?

WHAT'S IT LIKE TO LIVE HERE?
CITY
BY KATIE MARSICO

WHAT'S IT LIKE TO LIVE HERE? WHAT'S IT LIKE TO LIVE HERE?

Published in the United States of America by Cherry Lake Publishing
Ann Arbor, Michigan
www.cherrylakepublishing.com

Content Adviser: James Wolfinger, PhD, Associate Professor of History,
DePaul University, Chicago, Illinois
Reading Adviser: Marla Conn, ReadAbility, Inc.

Photo Credits: Cover and page 1, ©iStockphoto.com/spfoto; page 5, ©Luciano
Mortula/Shutterstock, Inc.; page 7, ©Thomas La Mela/Shutterstock, Inc.; page 9,
©DyMax/Shutterstock, Inc.; page 11, ©Elena Elisseeva/Shutterstock, Inc.; page 13,
©Ng Yin Chern/Shutterstock, Inc.; page 15, ©Sergei Bachlakov/Shutterstock, Inc.; page 17,
©Pavel L Photo and Video/Shutterstock, Inc.; page 19, ©Axel Lauer/Shutterstock; page 21,
©Song Heming/Shutterstock, Inc.

LIBRARY OF CONGRESS CATALOGING-IN-PUBLICATION DATA
Marsico, Katie, 1980– What's It Like to Live Here?:
City / by Katie Marsico.
    pages cm. — (Community connections)
Includes bibliographical references and index.
ISBN 978-1-62431-564-0 (lib. bdg.) — ISBN 978-1-62431-588-6 (ebook) —
ISBN 978-1-62431-580-0 (pbk.) — ISBN 978-1-62431-572-5 (pdf)
1. City and town life—Juvenile literature. I. Title.
HT119.M365 2014
307.76—dc23   2013025644

Cherry Lake Publishing would like to acknowledge the
work of The Partnership for 21st Century Skills. Please
visit *www.p21.org* for more information.

Printed in the United States of America
Corporate Graphics Inc.
January 2014

CITY

CONTENTS

BUSY MORNING

Charlie yawned. He liked waking up to the sounds coming from outside. Car horns honked. Engines zoomed. Charlie jumped out of bed to look out his window. Outside, huge buses rumbled down the street. Yellow taxis weaved between them. Tall skyscrapers towered in the distance. Charlie smiled. He loved growing up in the city!

Taxis are a common sight on city streets.

4

What city in the United States is home to the largest number of people? What city in Canada has the most people? If you guessed New York, New York, and Toronto, Ontario, you are right! New York is home to more than eight million people. Nearly three million people live in Toronto.

5

A city is an **urban** area. It is home to a large, **dense** population. Cities are crowded and busy **communities**. A lot of people share working and living space. **Residents** come from **diverse** backgrounds.

Some cities are home to millions of people.

What pets do city kids own? Dogs and cats are common pets. Families have to pick the right pet for city living, though. For example, keeping a very active dog in a small apartment is not always a good idea!

SCHOOL DAY

Charlie got ready for school. He grabbed his backpack and met his mom at the door. Together, they left their big apartment building. Most of Charlie's friends lived in apartments or **condominiums**. His friend Sophie lived in a **townhouse**. Like Charlie, these friends shared a yard or garden with their neighbors. Charlie did not know many kids with backyards of their own.

Apartment buildings are often several stories high.

ASK QUESTIONS!

Some apartment buildings have special rules to help neighbors get along. The rules help residents to be thoughtful about how much noise they make. Rules also help residents respect shared spaces. Talk to some people living in a city. What other rules do they follow?

9

Charlie and his mom headed for the train station three blocks away. The streets were filled with people going to work or school. Some people were just visiting the city for fun. Charlie heard people speaking Spanish and Cantonese. He did not recognize one language. "That family came here from India," his mom explained. "They are speaking Punjabi."

One fun winter activity that attracts visitors to many U.S. and Canadian cities is ice skating.

Think about all the
languages that are
spoken in cities.
People in Toronto
speak more than 140
languages. People use
some 800 languages
in New York City.

11

The train was packed when Charlie and his mom got on. They both had to stand until they reached their stop. After leaving the train, Charlie spotted Sophie. She had taken the bus to school. Charlie's friend Luis was just arriving on his bike, too. Charlie said goodbye to his mom and ran to catch up with them.

Trains and buses can be crowded in the morning, when many people are traveling to work or school.

Does everyone living in a city own a car? Not at all! Heavy city traffic makes driving a car difficult. Hopping on a train, bus, or trolley can be easier and cheaper. Sometimes kids live very close to schools and stores. They just walk or ride their bikes there!

13

EXCITING EXPERIENCES

The teacher Mr. Li started class with an activity. He asked the students to share something exciting they had done. Sophie said she had gone to a hockey game that weekend. She had rooted for their city's team. And they won!

Fans love to cheer on their home team.

LOOK!

Look at a map of your country. Try to find three or four major cities. Which one is closest to you?

15

Another student, Kyle, had visited a local museum. He got to see dinosaur skeletons. Luis talked about a play he had seen. The theater was only two blocks from his family's apartment. Luis and his family were able to simply walk there!

Some city museums offer a close-up look at dinosaurs.

LOOK!

Learn more about the cities that interest you. You could look for information online. You could also check out books from the library. Do you see pictures of any popular events or activities? Are there any cities you would like to visit?

Charlie talked about a festival he had visited. It celebrated South American **culture**. His aunt Alice had taken him to the event. It was set up along a street. Tents sold food and art. Musicians and dancers performed on stages.

Cities offer a variety of exciting festivals.

Do you have friends or family who live in a city? Ask them about it. What sights, sounds, smells, and tastes have shaped their lives?

19

JUST ANOTHER DAY

After school, Charlie went to swim class. He liked helping the younger kids learn to swim. Then his mom came to pick him up. At home, they had dinner. Charlie helped clean up the dishes. He did his homework and played video games. Finally, it was time for bed. Charlie went straight to sleep. Another busy day in the city!

Charlie was thrilled when he helped a younger kid learn not to be afraid of the water.

CREATE!

Think about day-to-day life in your favorite city. Create a picture of what you imagine. You can use crayons, colored pencils, paint, or markers. Include homes, schools, shops, and streets. Be sure to show popular attractions, too.

GLOSSARY

communities (kuh-MYOO-nut-eez) places and the people who live in them

condominiums (kahn-duh-MIN-ee-uhmz) apartment houses or other buildings in which each unit is owned by the person who lives in it

culture (KUHL-chur) the ideas, customs, traditions, and way of life of a group of people

dense (DENS) crowded or thick

diverse (dye-VURS) having many different types or kinds

residents (REZ-uh-dents) people who live in a particular place on a long-term basis

townhouse (TAUN-haus) a home that is part of a group of homes connected to each other by at least one wall

urban (UR-buhn) having to do with or living in a city

22

FIND OUT MORE

BOOKS

Boudreau, Hélène. *Life in a Residential City*. New York: Crabtree, 2010.

Lamprell, Klay. *New York City: Everything You Ever Wanted to Know*. Oakland, CA: Lonely Planet, 2011.

Smallman, Steve. *Santa Is Coming to Toronto*. Naperville, IL: Sourcebooks, 2012.

WEB SITES

BrainPOP Jr.—Rural, Suburban, and Urban
www.brainpopjr.com/socialstudies/communities /ruralsuburbanandurban/preview.weml
Learn more about life in different community settings, including country areas, suburbs, and cities.

Maps of World—North America Cities Map
www.mapsofworld.com/north-america/map-of-north-america.html
Check out this map to view major cities in Canada, the United States, and Mexico.

INDEX

ABOUT THE AUTHOR

Katie Marsico is the author of more than 100 children's books. She lives in a suburb of Chicago, Illinois, with her husband and children.